How to Understand
Auto Racing

WINTERNATIONALS

Lothrop, Lee & Shepard Books
New York

How to Understand
Auto Racing

Ross R. Olney

Lothrop Books by Ross R. Olney

How to Understand Auto Racing
Out to Launch: Model Rockets
Drama on the Speedway
The Young Runner
How to Understand Soccer
Tricky Discs: Frisbee Saucer Flying

With Chan Bush
Roller Skating!!

Title-page photo: Sometimes a top fuel dragster driver will apply too much power off the starting line, resulting in a "giant wheelie" as shown here. (*Ross R. Olney photo*)

Printed in the United States of America.
First Edition
1   2   3   4   5   6   7   8   9   10

Library of Congress Cataloging in Publication Data

Olney, Ross Robert (date)
How to understand auto racing.

Includes index.
SUMMARY: Examines racing cars, tracks, and the various automobile racing organizations.
1. Automobile racing—Juvenile literature.   2. Automobile racing—United States—Societies, etc.—Juvenile literature.   3. Automobile racing—Societies, etc.—Juvenile literature.   [1. Automobile racing]   I. Title   GV1029.0415   796.7'2
79-14558   ISBN 0-688-41913-5   ISBN 0-688-51913-X lib. bdg.

Contents

This Marmom Wasp is being driven by Ray Harroun to victory in the very first Indianapolis Speedway Race in 1911.

Introduction

The first real auto race was held between Paris and Bordeaux (and back to Paris) in France in June, 1895. The full distance of the race was 732 miles. It was won by Emile Levassor driving a Panhard/Daimler automobile. It took Levassor 48 hours and 47 minutes to cover the distance, giving him an average speed of 15.01 miles .per hour.

Auto racing was fairly simple in those days. You got a car and entered the event. Complications were few. People were even allowed to run across the track between racers (a few of them paid with their lives).

Modern automobile racing is a confusing mixture of types and tracks and clubs and terms. Can a Formula One car win at the Indianapolis Speedway?

No.

Why not?

Because the rules say so. A Formula One car, one of the finest racing cars in the world, doesn't meet Indy rules. But then, an Indy Championship car doesn't meet F/1 rules either.

What is a "stock car" and where can it race?

This Shaw Gilmore Special was driven by Wilbur Shaw to victory in the 1937 Indy race.

How can a tiny midget racing car beat a huge Formula 5000 car, now a Can Am racer? It all has to do with rules and regulations and clubs and tracks.

It doesn't really have to be hard to understand, either. Let's go step by step from the beginning to modern racers, clubs, and superspeedways.

The World Clubs

Many fans of auto racing couldn't care less about organizations. They come to races to see speed and color and excitement. If they want to worry about anything, they worry about ticket prices and mud in the infield. They worry about the cleanliness of the rest rooms and the taste and quality of the food at the concession stands.

But the organizations and clubs of auto racing exist in almost embarrassing profusion. Some clubs attempt to run certain parts of the sport. Some manage it. A few clubs raid one another for drivers. They quibble and bicker with one another over who is the boss. It is a sadly amusing sight to see them sniping away at each other. The fans are usually the last people they think about.

Each one would like to see the star drivers of the others come over to their races. Why? Because people will pay higher and higher ticket prices to see drivers like Mario Andretti, A. J. Foyt, Don Garlits, Richard Petty, and David Pearson. But Petty seldom races Andretti and Foyt never races Garlits. They are all in different clubs, in different types of racing.

(Goodyear phot

People will pay higher and higher ticket prices to see drivers like A. J. Foyt . . .

And ace woman driver Janet Guthrie . . .

(Ross R. Olney phot

(Ross R. Olney photo)

And all-around racing champion Parnelli Jones . . .

And world drag-racing champion Kelly Brown . . .

(Ross R. Olney photo)

And Richard Petty and David Pearson, even if they finish some of their races like this.

The associations and clubs jealously guard their positions in the sport. Sometimes they are their own worst enemies. They make rules that serve only to strengthen their own positions. The fans, the paying members of the second most watched sport in the world, come second.

An example? The United States Auto Club (USAC), a member of the world clubs, was secure in its Championship Division for years. With very few exceptions, everybody drove an Offenhauser-powered roadster. One year every single car in the field at the Indianapolis Speedway was almost identical. The engines *were* identical.

Some rear-engine cars showed up, but nobody thought they could win. So nobody worried. The rear-engine cars did very well and soon everybody had to design and build new rear-engine cars. This cost a great deal of money. It also made the front-engine roadsters obsolete.

So when Andy Granatelli came along, USAC was

When the little rear-engine cars came to Indy, it cost the owners of the big roadsters (rear car) a great deal of money.

(Indianapolis Motor Speedway photo)

So they were really shocked, and USAC was ready, when Andy Granatelli brought the strange, fat turbine to be driven by Parnelli Jones.

wary. Granatelli was known for bringing in strange and different racers. None had ever done very well, so they smiled and allowed them to compete. This time Granatelli shook the establishment hard. He brought a turbine-powered racer to Indianapolis. The car was within the rules, and it looked *fast*. What was worse, Granatelli hired former Indy winner Parnelli Jones to drive his strange, almost silent racer. Jones was not some wet-behind-the-ears rookie desperate to drive any car just to get to the famous Speedway. He was a proven member of the establishment. He wouldn't take a car if he didn't think it could win the 500-mile race.

The Granatelli-Jones racer "swooshed" to within a whisker of winning the 1967 Indianapolis Speedway Race. It dominated the entire field. The squat red car led most of the way and, with only eight miles to go, nobody was anywhere near it. Unfortunately for Jones and Granatelli, a small part failed and the car didn't finish.

Did that fact bother USAC's directors? No! They were ready this time. They voted to restrict the intake area of the turbine. This cut its power back, even though Granatelli's car met the requirements of the previous rules. Many of the directors were owners of traditional race cars. They didn't want to see their millions of dollars of investment go down the drain if the turbine won.

Granatelli fought them in court, but they won. So he came back with three more turbines under the *new* rules. They were less powerful, but Granatelli believed they could still compete. He also believed that Americans would soon be driving turbine-powered passenger cars if his cars won at the Speedway. Again, very near the end of the long race, one of them was leading. But again a small part failed in the fuel pump and the car lost.

Really frightened this time, the USAC board again met and again cut down on the turbine. This time they did it right, and no turbine-powered racer has returned to the Speedway. Development of cars and testing new things for passenger cars didn't concern them. Dollars, *their* dollars, did.

Fédération Internationale de l'Automobile (FIA)

The whole automobile shooting match is watched over by the Fédération Internationale de l'Automobile (FIA), based in Paris, France. It was formed as the International Association of Recognized Automobile Clubs in 1904. It has been called the "United Nations" of auto racing.

The FIA is a voluntary association of national auto clubs from seventy countries, give or take a few. The purpose of the FIA is to promote an exchange of ideas about automobiles and motor sports around the world.

Certain races in the United States (and around the world) are listed as having an "FIA sanction" or as being "listed" by the FIA. If a driver is licensed by the FIA (as most of the top driving stars are) he or she can compete in these races no matter what a local club might say. The Indianapolis Speedway Race (a USAC race) is FIA-listed. So Bobby Allison and his brother Donnie, NASCAR drivers but also FIA license holders, can participate—no matter what NASCAR says. Also, foreign drivers can drive in the United States FIA-listed events. Scotsman Jim Clark won the 1965 Indy race and Englishman Graham Hill won the same race in 1966 with FIA licenses.

All of this works on paper better than in reality, though. If NASCAR *really* doesn't want its drivers going over to race in the competition's events, they need merely sanction a major NASCAR race at the same time. Drivers can be made to compete in their own association races where there is a conflict.

Fédération Internationale du Sport Auto (FISA)

One section of the FIA is responsible for motor racing around the world. Remember, the FIA is interested in automobiles in general. This motor racing committee is called the Fédération Internationale du Sport Auto (FISA). It is the old Commission Sportive Internationale (CSI). The name was changed in 1979.

The FISA is made up of permanent members from Britain, France, West Germany, Italy, Japan, and the United States, plus twelve members elected from other FIA countries.

Always using the French language, this group draws up the actual rules for motor racing around the world. If there is a dispute, the judgment is rendered in the French language. This is the group that sets up an international racing schedule called the International Sporting Calendar. They attempt to see that major races around the world do not compete with one another on the same day (a Formula One race against the Indy race, for example). They also decide whether a race is big enough to be "listed" on their calendar.

In 1979, for example, the FISA noticed that the world-famous Long Beach Grand Prix was being planned for April 8. But there was another FIA race on April 8, a smaller and less important Formula Two race. One race was in Long Beach, California, U.S.A.; the other was in Hockenheim, Germany. Still, the FISA had the power to order the Long Beach Grand Prix promoters to pay $20,000 to the Hockenheim promoters before the April 8 date could be listed on the calendar.

The payment was supposed to be for the reduced crowd and field the Formula Two race would suffer as a result of the competition from Long Beach.

The FISA is the international group that oversees the Formula One races. Said by some to be the most dangerous of all races, these are events held in different countries around the world. The United States has two Formula One races. One is at Watkins Glen, New York, in the fall and one is at Long Beach, California, in the spring.

This series of races known as the "Grand Prix" determines a World Driving Champion of motor racing. The

Jody Scheckter lifts the right front wheel of his Formula One racer, one of the most sophisticated machines in the world.

The John Player Special of the late Ronnie Peterson is a Formula One car. These are under the direct supervision of the FISA (with the help of FOCA).

cars are smaller and lighter and with less power than an Indianapolis-type racer, but they are *lightning fast* on the road courses they race. They demand a driver of great skill and versatility. Only two Americans have ever become World Driving Champion. One was Phil Hill in 1961 and the other was Mario Andretti in 1978.

Local clubs in each country usually sanction and provide the workers for Grand Prix races, but the FISA is in overall charge.

Recently, however, the FISA has been "helped" with

Mario Andretti is only the second American driver to win the World Driving Championship (in 1978).

their Formula One races by an organization called FOCA (Formula One Constructor's Association). Some of the owners and builders of Formula One cars felt that they weren't getting the best deal they could from the earlier CSI. So they organized and dictated their terms to the Commission Sportive Internationale in the 1970s. CSI would play their way, or they would take their cars and go home. The battle for superiority has continued, even though the CSI has become the FISA.

A similar situation has developed in the United States

with an organization called CART (Championship Auto Racing Teams). CART is almost exactly the same in American racing as FOCA is in world racing. CART directs championship racing as FOCA directs Formula One racing. More about CART in the section on the United States Auto Club.

Who makes up the membership in FISA? Most countries have one single automotive club of note. This club represents that country on FISA. But this is not true in the United States. In the United States there are four major associations, representing four different types of motor racing.

There is the National Association for Stock Car Auto Racing (NASCAR), the Sports Car Club of America

Gordon Johncock (#20), a CART driver, passes Bobby Allison, who is a NASCAR driver, in the FIA-listed Indianapolis Speedway Race.

(SCCA), the National Hot Rod Association (NHRA), and the United States Auto Club (USAC). Then there are many, many smaller organizations such as the International Motor Sports Association (IMSA), SCORE International, and others. Some of them are growing quite powerful in their type of racing. IMSA, for example, runs more than thirty-six races per year for more than 1300 cars and pays out more than one million

The Top Fuel Dragster of Gary Beck is unloaded at the World Finals. Beck is an NHRA driver. NHRA belongs to ACCUS-FIA. ACCUS-FIA belongs to FISA and FISA belongs to FIA.

dollars in prize money. IMSA is an invited member serving on the FISA.

The four major racing clubs and others make up still another organization. This one has a very long name.

Automobile Competition Committee for the United States-FIA, Inc. (ACCUS)

The United States needed a representative on the world motor racing body, the FISA. But there were four different types of racing in the United States. So the four biggest clubs got together and formed a committee to represent them on the old CSI, now the FISA. It became the Automobile Competition Committee for the United States-FIA, Inc. (ACCUS).

Now ACCUS speaks for American racing on the FISA. FISA speaks for world racing to the FIA. The ACCUS is made up of the four member clubs (NASCAR, SCCA, NHRA, USAC) and others suggested by the four clubs, such as IMSA.

The U.S. Clubs

Most major automobile racing in the United States is controlled, guided, and managed by the four biggest clubs. These clubs were formed to oversee certain types of racing.

You can join these clubs if you like. You will receive a membership card and become a part of that type of racing, if you want to pay the dues.

But you will not control the racing. The club's leaders do that. Each club has a Board of Directors or other people to make the rules for their type of racing. Sometimes the drivers are included on these boards. Often the race car owners are included. Other officials are included, too. Sometimes even just people who like racing are on the board.

You can be a worker if you wish. Some clubs ask their members to help by handling flags on a corner at the race track. Or by manning a fire extinguisher (fire is a deadly danger to race car drivers).

It has happened that corner workers have saved the lives of racing drivers by quick action. If there is a crash on the track, the corner workers run to help. If a driver

(Ross R. Olney photo)

Some workers in U.S. clubs like NASCAR take a very active part, such as these pit workers servicing a car during a recent Los Angeles Times 500 at Ontario.

is trapped, they help get him out. If a car catches fire, they help put the fire out. If a driver needs an ambulance, they call it for him. Being a corner worker is a fine way to get involved in racing if you don't want to drive race cars.

Some people might work by waving the starting flag and the checkered flag. Other club members might help get news of the races in the newspapers. Others might sell programs or work in the pits. But most of the club

Other workers, shown here behind 1978 Cal 500 winner Al Unser and his car owner, Jim Hall, do other things at race tracks.

members in the big clubs just like to go to the races. They support that kind of racing by buying tickets and watching the races.

The four large clubs control four different types of racing. You've probably heard of all four, even if you didn't know what they did. Most of them have professional branches (or are all professional). The biggest-name drivers belong to these four clubs. Some of these drivers have made a great deal of money driving racing cars. A few of them have become millionaires.

The clubs help to arrange the races, license the driv-

The lonely corner worker (upper center, holding out flag) warns these SCCA Formula Vee racers of a problem on the track.

ers, and collect and pay out the money. If you go to a race, you are paying into a fund that will help pay the drivers for winning. This "purse" is often figured as a certain proportion of the money paid in by spectators.

The clubs also make the rules for their type of racing. They have people who inspect the cars to be sure they meet their rules. The president of a major racing club is a very powerful person in that type of racing.

Let's take a look at the different clubs.

National Association for Stock Car Auto Racing (NASCAR)

Many years ago people enjoyed racing their cars in fields all over the country. They would just lay out a track and start racing. This type of racing was especially popular in the southern part of the United States. Drivers and spectators just had fun.

Bashed fenders and broken radiators were often the results of one of these "cow pasture" races. There were no real rules. Anybody could race anybody else.

The cars were "stock." A stock car is a car that is basically the same as it was when it came off the assembly line. Nothing was done to the car to change it into a racing car. In fact, many of these old cars weren't good enough to run on the streets, so they raced in the fields. If a fender got bent, so what?

But don't think this was unskilled racing. It took real skill to win. Those early-day stock car drivers were learning how to handle their cars in competition.

"Stock" cars are not really stock at all. They are racing cars from bumper to bumper. Here Bobby Allison (#15) races with Richard Petty (#43) at Ontario Motor Speedway in 1978.

Janet Guthrie flashes past at nearly 200 miles per hour.

When stock car racing started, there was a law in the United States prohibiting the sale of alcoholic beverages. But many people during this "Prohibition" time still liked to drink whiskey, beer, wine, and other alcoholic drinks. And many of them continued to make "moonshine" at home. They would make enough for themselves and often enough for other people, too. So the bottles had to be hauled to the customers.

They were loaded into cars and delivered. But all of this was against the law, so federal officers were always watching for such deliveries. Very often when one was seen, a wild chase would result. The "moonshiner" would race his car along the back roads at night with no lights at all. He would scream around corners and race down straight stretches.

Not far behind would come the "revenooers" (Federal Internal Revenue officers) trying to catch the car with the illegal whiskey.

These drivers, if they didn't get caught and sent to prison, became very skilled at car handling. When they weren't hauling moonshine (or brewing it at their stills) they would join the races in the cow pastures. They just wanted to keep their driving skill at a razor edge.

Cow pasture races became more and more popular. People began to pay to come and watch. Then the drivers would split the money, with the winner taking the most.

It wasn't long before certain drivers became regular winners. They became very, very good at driving stock

This is a 1978 Thunderbird, and yet it is not a 1978 Thunderbird. It is a NASCAR stock car to be driven by Bobby Allison, and it is a race car pure and simple.

cars in races. Also, they began to do things to their cars to make them go faster. They would tune the engine very carefully, or even add parts.

But there were no real rules. Anybody could race anything. The rule then, in most races, was "run what you brung." If somebody really didn't like what you did, you would have to fight with fists out back of the barn to decide the winner.

Stock car racing was loose and easy. Of course, to grow into what it is today it needed somebody to take

NASCAR also sanctions older stock cars called Late Model Sportsmen. A group of them is shown here on the backstretch at Riverside in California.

over and lead. For there is no resemblance at all between today's rainbow-colored, thundering, high-speed stock cars and yesterday's cow pasture jalopies.

A man by the name of William H. G. France was visiting in Daytona Beach, Florida in 1934. He had a car problem and had to stay for a few days while his car was repaired. Bill France liked the little town and decided to settle there.

One of the reasons he liked it so much was because of the rough-and-tumble stock car races. They raced on the long, smooth beach in that town. France moved to Florida and joined in on the races.

One of the drivers he raced was Lee Petty. Petty became a famous stock car champion in a few years, but probably not as famous as his champion son still more years later.

It was 1947 before Bill France decided to organize the tough band of drivers into a club. He had a meeting with some of them at the Streamline Motel in Daytona Beach on December 14. They decided to call their club the National Association for Stock Car Auto Racing. It soon became known as NASCAR.

It was a grand name for a small group of cow pasture and beach drivers in beat-up old cars. The club grew, though. NASCAR became a powerful organization. It has by now paid out millions and millions of dollars in prize money to stock car drivers. NASCAR watches over some of the most competitive racing in all of motor sports.

There are other groups and clubs who run stock car races. NASCAR is the major club, the most important one by far. The most famous stock car driving stars drive for NASCAR.

Richard Petty, the son of Lee, is a NASCAR driver. So are David Pearson, Cale Yarborough, and Darrell Waltrip. Bobby Allison, his brother Donnie, and Benny Parsons are NASCAR drivers.

Of course the cars are not really "stock" anymore. You'll read in the section on race cars in this book that NASCAR stock cars are really race cars from bumper to bumper. But they still look something like stock cars and they are still called stock cars.

NASCAR runs the "Grand National" circuit of stock car races for late-model stock cars. These are long, difficult races on high-banked oval tracks (and one road course at Riverside, California).

NASCAR's first race was held on the beach at Daytona Beach on February 15, 1948. It was won by Red Byron. Bryon was paid real money for his victory, but not very much.

Today, cars that cost hundreds of thousands of dollars to design and build battle each other at speeds of nearly 200 miles per hour on high-speed superspeedways of NASCAR. This is thrilling racing, where fenders touch and two cars go spinning and bouncing crazily as smoke boils from tortured tires and car parts fly in all directions.

NASCAR sanctions races other than Grand Nationals. There is the Grand American series for older stock cars, and other series for modified stock cars. NASCAR races are held all over the country, at smaller tracks as well as the famous ones. But stock cars are their domain. They sanction races for smaller stock cars and older

In another instant, course workers are going to be on the scene with rescue equipment and fire equipment for these NASCAR stock car drivers.

stock cars and on a variety of dirt and paved tracks, but always stock cars.

Drivers now win hundreds of thousands of dollars in NASCAR racing. Richard Petty and Cale Yarborough have won *millions* of dollars. Other famous drivers have won almost as much. NASCAR is big business.

But it is still just one of the racing clubs you can join if you wish.

The author chats with Mario Andretti after Andretti has been forced to drop out of a NASCAR stock car race.

Sports Car Club of America (SCCA)

Wilbur Shaw, who was best known as an Indianapolis Speedway driver and finally as president of the Speedway, once attended a sports car race. He was shocked.

"All those *people*," complained the dapper Shaw, "and no admission charge. It's *murder!*"

That was in 1948 and sports car racers were casual. They just loved to race. They didn't worry about charging people to watch. Times have changed.

The Sports Car Club of America (SCCA) was formed by people who enjoyed road racing. They were am-

SCCA always leaned to sports car racing, like this B Production Porsche . . .

. . . or this B Production Corvette.

(Ross R. Olney photo)

SCCA allowed women to drive. Janet Guthrie, here crawl-ing into an Indy-type championship car, got her start in SCCA.

ateurs. They liked racing for the fun of it. They leaned to the European type of racing rather than American-as-apple-pie stock cars on oval tracks.

They would go out on weekends and race their little cars on roads, airport runways, or race tracks with road courses. They would obtain sports cars from overseas (most SCCA people didn't trust American cars). They would even allow *women* to race.

The first major organized SCCA race was on the streets and roads of Watkins Glen, New York, in 1948. The race was won by Frank Griswold, who was driving a pre-World War II Alfa Romeo. Griswold didn't win money; he won a trophy. But he was just as proud of his hard-earned trophy as many drivers are with a check.

SCCA is probably the most member-oriented of the auto racing clubs. They try to please their legion of members. The members have a voice in the rules. Many, many members take an active part in the races as drivers or workers.

Families attend the races to work on or drive the cars. Children run free in the paddock areas (but not in the

SCCA is member-oriented. This young woman driver is in the showroom stock class (note license plate on car).

(Ross D. Olney photo)

Duke Copeland, foot on the tire, drives. His sister Lisa, wiping the car, works on the pit crew.

pits). Very often there are more people in the garage area than in the grandstands.

SCCA racing was for pure fun. Yes, drivers were injured and even killed, for auto racing is dangerous at every level, but still it was for fun. To make competition as even as possible, many different classes of cars were recognized. In most years, more than 300 events were held across the country. At each event, many individual fields of cars would roar off in each separate race. Some-

The van is for sleeping and tool-hauling, and the whole family can participate in this Formula Vee effort.

times classes of cars were combined and there would be class winners as well as overall winners in each race. It was exciting racing for the people involved. It still is.

Doctors and lawyers and engineers and salesmen and anybody else able to afford a car for racing enjoy the competition. They even have classes for pure stock cars fresh off the showroom floor. You drive out to the race track, enter your car, race, then drive back home (hopefully).

Sometimes different classes of cars are combined into a single SCCA race.

In 1962 a major wave rolled through SCCA. Professional road racing was becoming very popular. The names of European drivers (and certain American drivers, too) were becoming familiar to race fans everywhere. It was obvious that somebody would soon be sanctioning *professional* road racing in America. Until then, the SCCA had been for amateurs, for "fun" racing.

It was against the wishes of many members. They spoke loudly against the plan. But finally a division of SCCA was created to handle professional racing.

It was different from family-style racing. This new division was slick and polished. Ticket prices were es-

(Al Behary photo)

SCCA's most popular professional division is the Can Am. This is driver Patrick Depailler in a Can Am racer.

(Ross D. Olney photo)

tablished. Race schedules were created and spectators were invited. SCCA operations in the professional division became big business. It worked, too—millions of dollars in prize money have been paid out by SCCA for professional road racing.

This is road racing, not oval track racing. That is the difference and the specialty of SCCA. A road course has short straightaways, long straightaways, and right- and left-hand corners (curves and turns are called corners in road racing).

Some of the other clubs and associations have wan-

SCCA Formula One street racing is dangerous. Here, James Hunt flies up behind Mario Andretti over another car—and out of the 1977 Long Beach Grand Prix.

(LBGP photo)

dered into road racing, but SCCA is the major one. They have not attempted any oval track racing to speak of.

Now SCCA has divisions to handle amateur racing and professional racing. You can still go out on a pleasant weekend with your race car and your family and participate. Usually the grandstands will be empty. In fact, spectators are not encouraged at these amateur races because of insurance problems. If you want to take part, you usually buy a pit pass and become a bit of the action.

SCCA also holds races where the grandstands are

SCCA is involved in the two Formula One races each year in the United States. The one at Long Beach, California, is held on the streets, as this air view shows.

(LBGP photo)

jammed with spectators who have paid for a costly ticket to watch world racing stars in action. They help oversee the Grand Prix Formula One races in the United States with all the famous European drivers (and World Champion for 1978, American Mario Andretti).

Although SCCA has not invaded the territory of other clubs (oval track racing, stock cars, drag racing, etc.), they are usually more willing to allow their drivers to race with other clubs. Thus the fans become the real winners.

More about the many racing divisions in SCCA later in this book.

National Hot Rod Association (NHRA)

In the 1920s most high-performance cars were being developed in Europe. But in the 1930s the trend changed. Young American auto enthusiasts were gathering wherever there was a flat spot with a straight line to make their cars go faster. These were usually stripped-down Model T and Model A Fords. The drivers were referred to as "hot rodders."

The usually young drivers had worked on their carburetors and cylinder heads to make them better. Some of them had invented new tricks for speed and performance. Many of the cars were driven to the dry lakes, the best places for this type of activity. There they were stripped of fenders, windshields, lights, and other excess items. Then they were raced on a straight track to see who could go fastest.

Car enthusiasts like the great Ken Miles (left) were gathering to see who could make their car go the fastest.

After the race, the parts were all reinstalled and the cars driven back home again.

In 1937, the first meeting of a group called the Southern California Timing Association was held. SCTA discussed things such as ambulance service at the speed trials, points systems to determine champions, and trophies. The group was made up of five car clubs in the Southwest. As more and more car clubs joined, SCTA became very important to hot rod people.

After World War II, when activity picked up again,

Modern "hot rods" still look very much like their counterparts of an earlier day.

a young driver by the name of Wally Parks was elected president of SCTA. The next year he was elected general manager. In 1949, while still involved with SCTA, Parks became the editor of a new magazine called *Hot Rod Magazine.*

His magazine grew to be the voice of hot-rodders all over the United States. Then a reader wrote a letter to the magazine:

"Why not have a national organization devoted to hot-rodding? Something like a national hot rod association?"

Parks and his publisher, and thousands of readers, liked the idea. The National Hot Rod Association was formed with Wally Parks, Marvin Lee, and Ak Miller as founding officers.

NHRA worked on safety standards, sanctioning, and many other hot rod activities. Gradually the club became most interested in drag racing, racing cars two by two over a quarter-mile straight-line course.

The club ruled that all cars must have roll bars to protect the driver. These are heavy steel bars that curve up and over the driving compartment to help in case of

A colorful variety of different types of cars compete in NHRA drag racing.

(Ross R. Olney photo)

a rollover. NHRA insisted that all cars have clutch and flywheel shields to keep parts contained in case a clutch or flywheel exploded. They said all drivers in NHRA events must wear a crash helmet. Safety continued to improve.

The first city-sponsored, NHRA-sanctioned drag meet was held at Pomona, California, in 1953. The chief of police helped with the arrangements. Now, many community service clubs are involved in drag racing (Lions, Kiwanis, Rotary, Jaycees, etc.).

The "instant sport" of drag racing (a race sometimes takes only 5 seconds or so) draws millions of fans today. A colorful variety of racers fill the pits. From Top Fuel dragsters through modern Funny Cars to Stock Cars

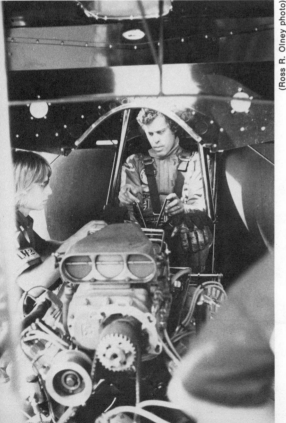

(Ross R. Olney photo)

Driver Don Prudhomme, one of the greatest in the history of drag racing, is known as "Snake." He is sitting in the cockpit of his Funny Car while a mechanic works.

with state license plates still attached, they gather. They are all there to settle one burning question.

With great sound and fury and smoking of tires and watering of eyes, who can cover the quarter mile fastest and quickest? Who can get to the end of the strip first? Who can be going at the highest rate of speed when they get there?

With noise so loud it hurts the ears (most experienced fans wear expensive earplugs), the two racers blast away at the flash of a green light. At the far end of the strip a light flickers in one lane or the other. This signifies the winner, the one to get there first. Everything is done by light beams and electronics so there are seldom any mistakes.

"The trick," said one fan about the loud noise, "is to keep your mouth open."

The drivers are known by such colorful names as Big Daddy, Cha Cha, the Snake, Mongoose, and Grumpy. Across the sides of the racers are lettered Black Magic, the Hawaiian, Rampage, Weekend Warrior, War Eagle, Checkmate, Quicksilver, Valley Fever, Blue Max, Motivator, Teacher's Pet, and other fanciful combinations.

Fans pay in millions of dollars to watch these gaudy, tremendously powerful cars make their quick runs.

Wally Parks remained as president of NHRA. There are rival groups like American Hot Rod Association and International Hot Rod Association who also sponsor major drag meets. Some of the champions in NHRA also compete in both AHRA and IHRA. But NHRA is

Since drag-racing fans are allowed in the area where cars are worked on, Blue Max's body protects the mechanics as they labor.

still the biggest and best-known club in drag racing. They pay the largest prizes and draw the most fans to races.

United States Auto Club (USAC)

Many years ago, the Indianapolis Speedway Race was sanctioned by the venerable American Automobile Association. So were the other races around the country for this type of "Indy" racer. Everything was labeled "AAA." The AAA provided the officials and timekeepers and starters.

Until 1955.

Primarily because of some very serious accidents in auto racing, AAA dropped out. They abolished their Contest Board, the group in AAA who had been governing the races. For a time, fans felt that nobody would rise to fill the gap. They didn't reckon with Tony Hulman. Hulman was the most current owner of the Indianapolis Speedway.

Big-time oval track racing, such as this race at Ontario Motor Speedway for Indy-type Championship cars, is under the sanction of USAC or, more recently, perhaps CART.

(Ross R. Olney photo)

Under Hulman's direction, a meeting was held. It became clear that big-league racing didn't need the AAA to survive. A board was chosen. The group of twelve people included drivers, mechanics, car owners, race promoters, and others. The group was named United States Auto Club, called USAC for short.

The board, now much larger and often under attack, continued to manage big-time oval track racing. They also created divisions for championship dirt track cars, sprint cars, midget cars, stock cars, land speed record cars, and other types of racing in the United States. Most

This "midget" racing car, with Mario Andretti preparing to drive, could beat a Formula One or an Indy car—but only on the midget's own race course.

people in racing recognize the well known USAC "shield." Of course there are other clubs who sanction oval track racing in the United States, dozens of them, but USAC is the biggest by far. And the most important. USAC belongs to ACCUS-FIA and none of the others do, in this type of racing.

USAC's main series or division was the "Championship Trail." This was a series of races on paved tracks across the country. It included the three major 500-mile races at Ontario, Pocono, and Indianapolis, the "triple crown" of auto racing. Championship Trail tracks are also located in Arizona, Wisconsin, Michigan, and several other states.

You can't miss an upcoming Championship Trail race in your area if you listen to the advertising on radio and TV. Ads will be heavy with the names of A. J. Foyt, Gordon Johncock, Johnny Rutherford, Janet Guthrie, Rick Mears, Tom Sneva, Danny Ongais, and other famous Indy-type race car drivers.

Sometimes World Driving Champion Mario Andretti raced in USAC races. USAC was Andretti's home club before he turned to world-class Formula One racing. Andretti has won the Indianapolis Speedway Race (in 1969).

The old AAA was filled with politics and judgments often questioned by fans and drivers alike. USAC has managed better, but not much better. Smaller groups were always arguing with the main body (typical in most forms of racing, but especially true with USAC).

Sometimes the results are unhappy. Here, Salt Walther's Indy-type car is hauled away after a crash into the wall of Ontario during the 1978 California 500.

On the other hand, they can be very happy. Wally Dallenbach celebrates victory with squirting champagne after winning the 1973 California 500 with an Indy-type racer.

In the sixties, USAC was shaken by an invasion of rear-engine cars from Europe. Here, A. J. Foyt (#1) chases Roger Ward in a new lightweight car. Foyt won the race at Indy that year.

One of the major threats came in 1978 when a group of car owners organized against USAC. Unhappy with certain regulations, they threatened to splinter off and run their own races.

They called themselves "CART" and suggested that they might be the new sanctioning body for Championship Trail racing. CART stood for Championship Auto Race Teams. It was true that within CART were many of the major names in that division of the sport.

Typically, USAC refused at first to talk seriously to the smaller group about their demands. So CART went

USAC also sanctions sprint cars such as this one being driven by A. J. Foyt at Ascot Speedway in Los Angeles.

off to find a new sanctioning body. They signed a contract with SCCA (so they would still have ACCUS-FIA sanction). SCCA said they would allow CART to handle Championship Trail races any way they saw fit. That was what CART wanted, to make their own rules to suit their own type of racing.

CART in the United States was just like FOCA in world-class racing. Both are groups of owners and drivers who feel they know more about their own type of racing than any board of directors who cover *all* types of racing.

What about USAC? Suddenly their most popular, money-making division was going to leave them. The somewhat stodgy, cantankerous, and slow-moving board had weathered other storms. It would weather this one. They fought back in their own way by threatening to allow stock engines in their races. This would mean that many new people could afford to race and would fill the gap left by CART.

To fans, it doesn't really matter who is in charge just so the big-name drivers and the fast cars are there. Whether USAC or CART sanctions Championship Trail racing (or whether they *both* do) is no problem to the fans. This type of auto racing will continue one way or the other. Auto racing in general has become the number two spectator sport in the United States. Number one is horse racing, with gambling allowed.

And midget racing cars such as this one that was just driven to victory by Bill Vukovich, son of the great Bill "Mad Russian" Vukovich. Famous race promoter J. C. Agajanian is wearing his trademark, a cowboy hat.

Each of the groups or clubs makes the rules for its type of racing. They provide the officials, see that the rules are obeyed, sell the sanctions to the race promoters, and oversee the races. They judge when problems arise. The clubs are very important to the smooth operation of auto racing.

Many modern racing fans don't see the need for such organization. The organizations cross over into each other's territory, overlapping in types of racing and competition for drivers. They threaten and cajole, attempting to protect their own interests. More often than not, they refuse permission for drivers to cross over. This hurts the programs and keeps extra action and racing excitement from the fans.

Yet the clubs are needed because today's racing world has grown so complex. In NHRA, for example, there are more than 100 different classes of cars. Most of them compete on the same weekend at the same track. *Somebody* has to be in the tower to keep things from getting all mixed up.

If an FIA license truly gave international permission to race in any FIA event, things would be smoother. Often it does work that way, but organizations still resist one another.

Smaller Clubs Also Compete

The International Motor Sports Association is a large auto club, but it is not as large as NASCAR, SCCA,

NHRA, or USAC. Still, IMSA runs many races each year. They sanction GT car racing. These are powerful sports cars like Porsche, BMW, Corvette, and others. This is endurance racing, with longer races but still with series-produced cars. The rules allow and encourage the entry of private teams. In some races, the cars are turbocharged (see the USAC car section) and in others they are not. The series is called Winston GT Challenge.

IMSA also sanctions stock cars in a series called the Champion Spark Plug Challenge. These racers are Datsuns, Mazdas, small Buicks, Gremlins, and the like.

Finally, IMSA sanctions a series called the American

IMSA style racing includes these modified Porsche cars for endurance races. This is the winning Watkins Glen 6-hour race car of P. Gregg, T. Hezemans, and P. Fitzpatrick.

Volkswagen of America photo)

Challenge for cars like the Nova, the Datsun 510, and other somewhat larger stock cars.

SCORE International, a California-based club, has off-road races. These are zany events with cars from many different classes competing on rugged trails and desert courses. This type of racing is becoming more and more popular, and eventually these owners and

Off-road racing has become more and more popular with fans and SCORE International is the main club.

(Ross R. Olney photo)

(Photo courtesy of Mickey Thompson)

Mickey Thompson (right) was most responsible for bringing off-road racing to its present popularity. He often co-drives with his son Dannie (left).

Off-road racing is hard, rugged, dirty work, but drivers say it is great fun.

(Ross R. Olney photo)

(Ross R. Olney pho

Off-road racers are off the ground as often as they are on it.

drivers will certainly bring their ideas to national and international level clubs.

There is the Formula Atlantic series, a Canadian-bred training ground for young road racers looking upward. These are open-wheeled, open-cockpit racers with Ford-based engines much like the European Formula Two (which is also a training ground for drivers hoping eventually to compete in Formula One).

Then there is kart racing. The International Kart Federation and the World Kart Association are two clubs sanctioning kart racing. Karts are tiny little platforms with a one-cylinder motor and a centrifugal clutch. They compete in three divisions: Sprint, Speedway, and Enduro, depending on length of race and type of track. They are small but very fast.

There are literally hundreds of smaller auto clubs. There is the United Racing Club for open-wheeled rac-

Formula Atlantic racing is said to be a training ground for young racers on the way up in road racing.

(Ross R. Olney photo)

These Formula Atlantic racers negotiate a tight hairpin turn during a race on the streets of Long Beach, California.

ers, the American Speed Association for stocks, the Automobile Racing Club of America for stocks, the United Auto Racing Association for midget racing cars, the Northern Auto Racing Club for sprints, the American Speed Association for late-model sportsmen, the California Racing Association for midgets and sprints, and the American Racing Drivers Club for midgets.

There is ARTGO, CORA, CAR, ATQMRA, MARFC, DIRT, NCRA, BMARA, RMMRA, AAARA, and many,

California Racing Association sprint car driver Dick Zimmerman four-wheel drifts around a corner at Ascot Speedway during a night race.

many more. There is the Auto Racing Fraternity Foundation (ARFF), a group which maintains a fund to be used for drivers in need. There are dozens and dozens of pure fan clubs as well, each one devoted to a certain race driver.

There is no reason why you or anyone else couldn't form a club for any kind of racing. It would then be up to you to organize, create a set of rules for your type of racing, and arrange for one or more race courses. It would be up to you whether or not "your" drivers could race in any other club's races.

In the cases of NASCAR, SCCA, NHRA, and USAC, and a few of the smaller clubs, the organizations grew into powerful clubs. They became clubs that controlled a large segment of a very popular sport.

Outside Sponsors

Racing does not survive on ticket sales. Modern auto racing is very, very expensive. Even the so-called cheaper forms of racing will cost a lot of money. The amateur types of racing are still expensive.

From individual drivers to the major clubs, people look for sponsors to put money into their type of racing. A brand-new Formula Vee driver might get the local VW dealer in town to chip in with a few spare parts. For this the driver will paint the name of the dealer on his car.

The driver gets a little financial relief and the sponsor gets his name in front of a crowd of race fans. If the driver keeps winning, he might get the sponsor to put more into the car. After all, the sponsor's name is being seen more if the driver is getting his picture into the local paper.

A club might seek a sponsorship for an entire series of racing. NASCAR's Winston Cup Series of racing is sponsored by Winston cigarettes. Winston also sponsors

Sponsors who are putting money into this F/5000 car of Mario Andretti are plain for all to see.

NHRA drag racing, IMSA racing, and other events. Sponsorship costs the company hundreds of thousands of dollars.

When USAC needed a sponsor for their Championship Trail, they went to First National City Traveler's Checks. A deal was made, and the Citicorp Cup was created. Again, hundreds of thousands were invested by Citicorp in a variety of services. But for all the expenses, they got to have their name on cars and on drivers' uniforms. It was difficult to get a photo without a Citicorp seal on it.

Sponsors of major-league auto racing come in a wide variety of types. Not all of them are involved in the auto business either, as the sponsorship from Citicorp indicates. But many of them are in the business.

Goodyear Tires, Valvoline Oil, Monroe Shock Absorbers, Champion Spark Plugs, and STP Oil Treatment are major auto-racing sponsors. Robert Bosch Corporation (spark plugs) is a major sponsor, and so are Volkswagen of America and Union Oil Company.

Companies not involved in the auto business have found auto racing to be a fine billboard for their prod-

In drag racing, sponsors plaster their decals all over the sides of the "high-speed billboards."

(Ross R. Olney phot

Even in sophisticated Formula One racing, sponsors are obvious. This is the odd six-wheeled 1977 Elf F/1 of Patrick Depailler.

ucts. Winston is only one. Gould, Inc., is a maker of electrical products for home and industry. They spend millions on auto-racing sponsorship. Sugaripe Prunes spend a great deal of money on racing. North American Van Lines is a major sponsor. Ingersoll-Rand Tools is heavily involved. Foreman Industries, Gilmore Broadcasting, Bryant Heating and Cooling, the Machinist's Union, Oberdorfer, Budweiser and Busch beers, Dayton-Walther Steel, Wendy's Hamburgers, ThermoKing, Norton Company, and Kelly Girl are all deeply involved. Norris Industries spends a lot of money in auto racing.

71

These sponsors, and many hundreds more at all levels of racing, put money into the sport because of the advertising and publicity they can get out of it. Many of them spend a lot and get very little in return, for the companies just love the sport.

Sponsors are a part of the lifeblood of auto racing. They help it to survive at the very expensive level it has reached.

Put Them All Together and They Spell Confusion

So it all works like this. The FIA is in charge of everything to do with cars in the world.

The FIA has a committee called the FISA. This committee is made up of car clubs involved in motor racing from around the world. The FISA specializes in competitive auto racing.

(Gould, Inc., photo)

Drivers, too, are walking billboards. This is 1977 and 1978 National Driving Champion Tom Sneva in his fire-resistant uniform.

Because the United States has several major car clubs involved in several different kinds of racing, some of them got together to make up the ACCUS-FIA, Inc. This American group has members from NASCAR, SCCA, NHRA, and USAC, and from other clubs like IMSA.

The ACCUS-FIA, Inc., is the United States member of the FISA. This is a committee of the FIA. So we are back where we started.

Most of the men and women important to auto racing in the United States are on the boards of one or more of these groups. They make the rules that filter down to the individual racers.

If you want to go out and race in a Formula Vee you must join SCCA. They handle all types of Formula road racing.

What it all amounts to is this: if you want to go out and race in Formula Vee, you join SCCA. This is the author's son, Ross D. Olney.

(Al Behary photo)

If you want to be an Indy driver, you must join USAC or CART. They handle oval track racing in the United States, at the major level. If you want to drag-race, NHRA (or AHRA or IHRA) is the place to apply. For the important stock car races, it's NASCAR. For endurance racing with series-produced sports cars, go to IMSA. For off-road racing, go to SCORE International.

You say you just aren't a "joiner"?

Then forget about auto racing in the United States. These, and all the smaller clubs, have it all sewed up.

The Cars
and the Tracks

NASCAR Stock Cars and NASCAR-Type Tracks

In NASCAR and all the other clubs, the rules are very strict.

"Run what you brung" has long since faded into the past. You will "run" what they say you can run, and not a fraction more or less. Unless you find a way to cheat—and that, too, is a part of auto racing.

Cheating on the technical rules is not really considered dishonest. It is all part of the game. If you can find a place to put an extra tank of fuel, for example, you might try. If the inspectors find the tank, you will be fined. It is possible they could ban you from the race.

One year it was found that nitrous oxide, "laughing gas," made an engine more powerful when it was injected into the carburetor. But it was against the rules to do anything like that. So some drivers figured out ways to hide nitrous oxide and feed it into the engine.

Some hid a small tank somewhere in the car. Some of the really tricky ones pumped the gas into their roll bars or some other well-hidden place. Then, during the race, when they needed an extra shot of power, they had a way to feed it into the engine.

A slight difference in body shape can give a real advantage to a driver. But the car must conform to certain standards. Inspectors have "body templates" to hold against the car before each race. Another way of bending the rules stopped.

The rules say the car must sit at a certain height off the track. But drivers knew that a lower car would go faster. So they figured ways to make the car stand up during inspection, then drop down during the race. They used things as simple as charcoal wedged into the shock absorbers. The first hard "squat" during the race would crush the charcoal and the whole car would settle down to where the driver wanted it.

NASCAR Grand National racers and most "stock" cars from other clubs are not really *stock* at all. Stock means that the car is just the way it was when it came off the assembly line at the factory. Nobody believes that a NASCAR Grand National stock car is anything at all like the way it was built at the factory.

They are *nothing* like the factory models they are supposed to represent (at the Grand National level). They are racing cars, pure and simple. From the ground up they are built as racing cars, but they are made to look like a factory model—and they do use the same engine, much modified.

They look like the factory model until you get close up. Then even the most casual car owner can see the

Nobody believes that this NASCAR "stock" car is truly stock, the way it came off the assembly line.

The inside of a NASCAR Grand National stock car, such as this one of Buddy Baker, has been gutted and refitted for racing.

difference. They look longer and lower and sleeker than their factory cousins (even though most of the measurements must remain the same). And of course the inside of the car has been gutted, with a bucket seat the only furniture.

Before every race, inspectors look over every car. They even remove the carburetors to see whether they are legal. Crew chiefs and drivers stand around looking either very calm or very nervous during these inspections. It doesn't matter. The calm ones could be cheat-

Careful inspection by trained people assures that every car, such as this one shown in a pit stop, is legal when it starts the race.

(NASCAR photo)

ing and the nervous ones could be legal in every respect. So the inspectors just go about their duties with their measuring equipment.

From there, the car is taken directly to the pits. It doesn't go back to the garage until after the race.

NASCAR racing is a colorful world of southern drawls, Confederate flags, good ol' boys (as the drivers are called), 200 miles per hour with fenders inches apart, and superspeedways banked so high you can't walk up the corners. It is pre-race prayers for the drivers, the smell of hot engines and hot rubber, southern belles in incredibly tight clothing, people who sometimes look dumb and slow, but who are smarter, quicker, smoother, and richer than most of the fans in the grandstands.

NASCAR racing is a wild blend of huge, bellowing cars and soft-spoken, countrified drivers who bring their families along and who go to church on Sunday. These are men and women who take part in their communities, who run for office and share in the taxes in towns such as Avery's Creek, Walnut Cove, Level Cross, Ellerbe, Hueytown, Randleman, and Inman.

They go by their first names. Everybody in racing knows Richard, Cale, Bobby, David, and Benny. They are familiar if somewhat stand-offish people. They want to be friends, but they still seem to have a mild mistrust of outsiders. Outsiders are from anywhere but the Deep South. They are "Jaws," "Coo Coo," "Hoss," "Gray Fox," and the "Alabama Gang."

NASCAR drivers like superstar Richard Petty are people who take part in their communities. Petty is a County Supervisor back home in North Carolina.

Their racing cars might look like those in the parking lot. They are *anything but*. Beginning with a new frame, they work them over in their racing shops on their farms in the South. Then they haul their cars in giant semi-trailers (or, if the budget isn't large, behind tow cars) to tracks like Daytona in Florida, Talladega in Alabama, Richmond in Virginia, Bristol in Tennessee, North Wilkesboro in North Carolina, Atlanta in Georgia, or other southern superspeedways. Sometimes they venture away from home to places like Brooklyn, Michigan, or Ontario, California, or Pocono, Pennsylvania, or Riverside, California. The whole "circus" of dozens of cars and teams arrives.

At these places the hired track band almost always favors them with a rendition of "Dixie" just to make them comfortable.

Then they race. It is the same people (with perhaps a few local stock car heroes in the field) racing against the same people. The races are almost always hard fought and fender to fender. Bashing into each other

A happy winner of the 1978 Los Angeles Times Grand Prix for NASCAR stock cars is Bobby Allison, another super-star stock car driver.

just the way their daddies used to do in the corn fields is still quasi-legal. At the end, one of them, usually from within the same group of four or five, will have won. The local heroes, almost without exception, will not have won. Then the whole gang of them will load up and move on to the next race, taking their gate money with them.

NASCAR racing at any level, from dirt bullrings where the not-yets and the has-beens are battling it out to see who will survive, to the superspeedways, is great racing. The crowds come, and enjoy.

There are other, smaller stock car clubs. Even stodgy USAC has a stock-car division. But NASCAR stock car racing is easily the best. They have the stars. They have the most exciting racing. They are by far the most popular.

NASCAR is the largest and strongest stock car racing organization in the world.

SCCA Cars and Tracks

Many members of the Sports Car Club of America might tend to sniff down their noses at the good ol' boys from NASCAR. In the first place, SCCA was built on the premise that Europeans made better cars than Americans. If a car was not smaller, sleeker, with four-on-the-floor and a whole row of carburetors, it wasn't as good.

SCCA members love smaller cars, rather than the

bellowing and snorting Dodges and Chevrolets and Oldsmobiles. SCCA racers don't usually sweat and they don't swoon and gasp for oxygen at the end of a grueling 500-mile race. In fact, they don't believe in grueling races at all. Not at the amateur level and not in spirit, at least.

Most of them are amateurs. It is slightly dishonest, in their view, to make a living from a sport like motor racing. That's what they call it, not "auto" racing. They'll walk a mile for a trophy with a little car on top, but to take *money*? My *goodness*!

In fact, SCCA racing at all levels can be rugged work. Since it is amateur racing, it is weekend-and-nights-after-work racing. Racers from all walks of life hurry home in the evening, grab a quick bite, then head for the garage. They must "work on the car." This becomes a way of life. If they are lucky, their family is with them. In some cases, the husband drives and the wife works on the car. In other cases, the wife drives and the husband is the mechanic. Sometimes they take turns, or do what feels right at the time. Some racers are whole-family projects.

An investment in a race car at the amateur level can still be substantial. It all started with a little fun racing on weekends. Americans are competitive people. They want to win. To them, losing is embarrassing.

So one driver invested a little more. Since SCCA is very particular about their rules, this was done within those guidelines. Perhaps the driver purchased a some-

A racing Corvette is a very expensive machine, tending to take a lot of time and a lot of money to maintain and race.

what more expensive set of spark plugs. With the new plugs, the race was won. Others, then, were face to face with a decision. Should they invest in the new, more expensive plugs, or should they run with the back-markers who won't?

The costs began to climb.

A modern Formula Vee racer—the single most popular class of auto racing in all of racing, in all of the world, in all of history—should not cost an arm and a leg. This class is said to be "everyman's" racing. You can have a modest job, it is said, and be a Vee racer at the SCCA club level. On paper, yes. But if you want to be a Vee *winner*, you are going to have to put your heart and soul and bankroll into the car, and probably mortgage the house, too.

SCCA club-style racing will eat you up. It will take

This SCCA H Production racer is a joy to its owner.

(Al Behary photo)

every minute of your time and every extra dollar of your money. Take Formula Vee again as an example. You can buy a whole Volkswagen engine for a few hundred dollars. It can be less than the cost of a single Indy-type racing crankshaft. But not a *winning* VW engine. A winning engine has been worked over by an expert. It has been ported and rebuilt to exact tolerances. Every extra horsepower counts when you are starting with only fifty. So the cost of the engine can easily climb to $3000 or more. That's for a *VW* engine.

The body and frame can be built at home, but winners are usually bought from companies who build winning bodies and frames. How much? Another couple of thousand, at least. Accessories? How much can you afford? You have to buy gas tanks and suspension systems and tires and wheels and many other components.

One meeting with the wall can wipe it all out. There is no car insurance in amateur racing. You eat your losses. You might find yourself wishing you had eaten them in food in the first place (instead of all those lunch meat sandwiches and beans). Still, thousands of drivers love this type of racing. So do their families.

SCCA amateur racing is broken into many different classes (including the popular Formula Vee). The club tries to make motor racing available to every member. Here are just a few of the classes:

Showroom Stock A (Datsun, Porsche, Mazda, Mustang, etc.). G Production (Spyder, Sprite, Spitfire,

There is no insurance in car racing. If this SCCA Formula A driver hits the wall, the expense of rebuilding is his alone.

etc.). Formula Ford (open-wheel racing car with Cosworth engine). A Sedan (Camaro, Cuda, etc.). A Production (Corvette, etc.). C Production (Datsun 280Z, Porsche, Lotus Elan, etc.).

There are many, many more classes and types of racers. The number of divisions in this one club alone is dizzying.

In the amateur division of SCCA, money can be earned. Some companies put up money for racers for one reason or another. Volkswagen of America, for example, pays modest purses to drivers in the Formula Vee class if they do well. Certain other drivers can earn

Dr. Fred McClung is the driver of this SCCA C Production racer.

money through amateur racing even though the class they race in is called amateur.

SCCA also has a professional division involved in "big time" motor races. The most notable of these, when SCCA works directly with FISA, are the two Formula One Grand Prix races each year. One is held at Watkins Glen, New York, and the other at Long Beach, California. The United States is the only country in the world with *two* F/1 races each year. Most countries have only one, and many countries have none though they would like to participate.

These races are for world class drivers. The most famous racing drivers in the world compete in the Grand Prix. The cars are ultra-sophisticated, open-wheel, open-cockpit missiles admirably designed to race on road courses. They are one-of-a-kind racers, used only for

Formula One races like this one at Long Beach, California, are for world-class drivers like Niki Lauda in this Ferrari.

Or World Champion Mario Andretti, shown here before the race with his car owner, Colin Chapman.

Or Ronnie Peterson, who died in a 1978 crash at Monza in Italy.

Or Alan Jones, who lost all stability in his car after a rather minor crash with another racer that bent his front wings.

this type of racing. They are very, very expensive, costing millions of dollars to design, build, and compete. Racing teams travel the world from Japan to Germany to South America to the United States and more, to race in the Grand Prix races. From these races a World Driving Champion is selected on the basis of points earned in each race.

In the United States it is the SCCA who handles details, provides officials and workers, and does the other groundwork for Grand Prix races (in cooperation with FISA and FOCA).

Formula One racing is fast, exciting, and very dangerous. The car of Patrick Tambay leaps over the car of Niki Lauda (#5) at the start of the 1979 Long Beach Grand Prix.

The professional division of SCCA also sanctions races known as Can Am and as Trans Am. Then they sanction a professional series for Super Vee racers (faster and more sophisticated Vee racers with water-cooled engines) called the Bosch VW Gold Cup. These cars are like USAC's Bosch Mini Indy racers.

It all started innocently enough, this SCCA pro division.

Word was filtering back from Europe about the great excitement of open-wheeled cars on road courses. Names like Jim Clark, Graham Hill, Jackie Stewart, and Bruce McLaren were ringing out in the racing world. Formula One had always been popular at its single appearance at Watkins Glen (the Long Beach Grand Prix came later, beginning in 1976). A few American drivers had tried it. Only one, Phil Hill, had won the World Driving Championship, in 1961.

SCCA had always raced on road courses, with right-hand and left-hand corners. They knew where the road courses were and how to deal with the owners. They had scheduled many, many amateur road races at these tracks.

The SCCA professional division started innocently enough with these Formula 5000 racers, this one driven by Jody Scheckter of later Formula One fame.

(Ross R. Olney photo)

And also these unlimited sports cars in the Canadian-American Challenge Cup series. This one was the all-time best, a Porsche-Audi driven by Mark Donohue.

So they decided to start a professional series of road races in the United States. They wanted it as near to European-style racing as possible. They started with a Formula A series, using open-wheel, open-cockpit racers with a standard American engine (usually Chevrolet) tuned for racing.

The Formula A racers were low and sleek and very fast. The A series of racing became popular. Crowds of spectators came to watch the hotly contested races. New American driving stars were born. One driver had only had a little experience in closed sedans, yet he became a Formula A champion and very well known. His name was Ron Grable.

David Hobbs, Peter Gethin, and other famous drivers from Europe came over to drive in America's new Formula A series. Formula A was the series that really got

94

Another Porsche-Audi driven by George Follmer.

professional road racing going with the SCCA. The series spread to Europe, South Africa, New Zealand, and Australia (as Formula 5000, with the same size engine and same specifications). Eventually it became known as Formula 5000 in the United States, too.

SCCA also sanctioned a professional series known as Can Am (Canadian-American Challenge Cup) that was very popular with fans. These huge, bellowing, high-speed Porsche and McLaren and other unlimited sports cars were magnificent. Mark Donohue was a great champion in this series, and so were Bruce Mc-Laren, Dennis Hulme, George Follmer, and Peter Revson.

But eventually, in the mid-1970s, both Formula 5000 (the old Formula A) and Can Am became so expensive to run that competition disappeared. The teams with enough money became the winners. Everybody else lost.

(Ross R. Olney photo)

The start of a Can Am race was a thunderously exciting moment.

SCCA still runs a Can Am series of races. Formula 5000 (the old Formula A) was very popular. So was the unlimited sports car Can Am series. So they combined the two, in a sense. They just put fenders and

The new Can Am series of SCCA is a combination of the two old ones. These are Formula 5000 cars with Can Am bodies.

sleek bodies on F/5000 cars, and called them Can Am cars. The new Can Am series became very popular with fans.

SCCA also sanctions a Trans Am series for professional racers. This is a series for modified sports cars like the Porsche, the Datsun, and the Corvette. These cars are very similar to the IMSA Winston GT (formerly Camel GT) racers.

Finally, SCCA is involved in a professional series

SCCA racing includes the usually tame VW Rabbit, several

(Volkswagen of America photo)

called Rabbit-Bilstein. This is a series of races for VW Rabbits.

Many of the more modern race tracks have more than one possibility for course layout. Perhaps an association wants to race on an oval, so the track can be blocked off in a certain way to provide an oval. Then along comes

shown here in Rabbit/Bilstein Cup racing.

another association and they want to race on a road course. Barriers can be moved and a road course of the right length is ready.

Riverside International Raceway in California is a popular track with SCCA because it has many possible configurations. Riverside has thirty-seven different course layouts.

Other famous race tracks used mostly by SCCA are Sears Point in California, Lime Rock in Connecticut, Ontario in California, Mid-Ohio in Ohio, Laguna Seca in California, and Road Atlanta in Georgia, where the big series of amateur championships is held each year.

All of these tracks have road courses. Many of them are used by other associations as well. USAC uses some of them, NASCAR uses some of them, IMSA uses some of them, even NHRA (drag racing) and SCORE (off-road racing) use some of them.

NHRA Cars and Tracks

Did you know this? You could speed your family car up to one hundred miles per hour and roar past a standing Top Fuel Dragster. The instant you pass, the dragster driver "burns out."

In *one quarter mile* (only 1350 feet) he would roar around you and be far ahead. That is how quickly these NHRA (and AHRA and IHRA) racers speed away from a standing start.

They are the top class in drag racing. They are long,

Riverside International Raceway in the high desert country of southern California is a popular track because of its many configurations.

Ontario Motor Speedway in California has an oval track with a road course inside, in the infield.

skinny, ungainly-looking racers that appear to be all engine and rear tires. The driver sits just in front of the engine (thanks to Don "Big Daddy" Garlits, who was seriously injured in an earlier front-engine model). When the lights on the Christmas Tree starting device turn green, they storm away to see which of the two racers can get to the other end of the straight line first.

102

They gulp a methane fuel mixture faster than the water runs out of your shower at home. They are often going 250 miles per hour at the end of their 5+-second run.

Like Indy cars, Formula One cars, and many other racers, dragsters have "wings." But they aren't for flying. In fact, they are upside-down wings. The wings create a downward force, holding the car firmly against

This Top Fuel Dragster of Jeb Allen could pass the family car in only a quarter-mile even though the car might have a 100 m.p.h. head start.

the track so that tires have as much "bite" as possible. If a wing flies off a car while it is in action, it almost always spins out and crashes. The wings on a racing car are very important. With the latest F/1 racers, the entire car is a wing. These are called "ground effect" cars.

Another popular division in drag racing is the Funny Car class. These rockets on wheels look something like a standard car, but then again they don't. They are lower and much sleeker. They seem to bulge in the wrong places. They have a huge supercharger air intake projecting up through the hood. The supercharger forces more air into the engine for more power. The driver sits back where the rear seat used to be.

Another popular class in NHRA drag racing is the Funny Car class.

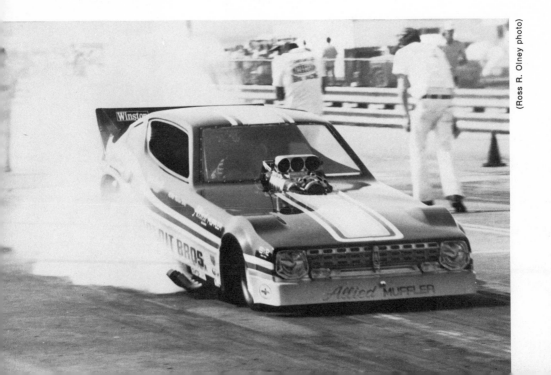

(Ross R. Olney photo)

Under the fiberglass replica of a modern American car is little more than a front-engine Top Fuel Dragster.

Funny Cars blaze away from the line with great sound and fury. Both Funny Cars and Top Fuel Dragsters can cover the quarter mile in six seconds, more or less, and reach top speeds of more than 240 miles per hour.

There are many, many other classes in drag racing. There is a class for everybody, including one for pure stock cars just like the ones out in the parking lot. Three of the classes are for professional drivers who earn a living at drag racing. These are Top Fuel Dragsters, Funny Cars, and Pro Stock cars.

There are many, many other classes, including these Pro Stock Dragsters, in NHRA drag racing. See the front end bounce off the ground when the driver hits the gas.

(Ross R. Olney photo)

Pro Stock cars are very near stock but with a number of speed modifications. They look almost like a real stock car. But they are much, much faster. Though they have the same engine and body as the auto they appear to be, they have been worked over, within the rules, to make them fast.

Pro Stockers are one of the favorites of the fans at a drag race because they are more nearly like the cars the fans drive.

The amateur classes of modern drag racing are called Sportsmen classes. There are Pro Comp, Competition, Modified, Super Stock, and Stock. Progressing upward from the Stock class, the racers are more and more modified and faster and faster. But still they are Sportsmen racers, not professionals. They can earn money at some of the events, but they really race for the fun of it.

In regional races across the country, the Sportsmen classes compete against each other. Each region winds up with a champion and some runners-up. These drivers race each other at the annual World Finals at Ontario Motor Speedway in California to see who is the World Champion in each class.

Only the drivers who finish among the top five in points within one of NHRA's seven geographic divisions are eligible to compete at the World Finals. In other clubs and associations (AHRA and IHRA, mainly) they have similar routes to the championship. Often, in fact, it is the same drivers and cars competing.

Meanwhile, the top three professional classes are competing in a series of national events. These, under the sanction of the NHRA, are called the Summernationals, the Springnationals, the Grandnationals, the Cajunnationals, the U.S. Nationals, and others. Competing sanctioning clubs sometimes name their big races in a similar fashion (Summer Nationals, etc.) but only in NHRA is it one word.

There are drag strips all over the country. They are anything from a simple quarter-mile of pavement (and lately even sand) to expensive tracks with every luxury. At one end is a starting line; at the other, exactly one-quarter mile away, a finish line. There is a way to time the cars during their run. This is usually done with electric light beams the car breaks at the beginning

Cars are timed in NHRA drag racing by electronic light beams and clocks. The wheels break one beam to start, and another at the finish line to complete the race.

and at the end. An electronic clock measures the interval.

But a drag race can be handled by a flagman and a timer with a stopwatch. That is how it was always done not that many years ago.

Women began making inroads in the sport of auto racing years ago. This was especially true in the SCCA, where women drivers were always welcome. But in NHRA drag racing is the only woman World Champion. Shirley Muldowney won the top championship in the top class, Top Fuel Dragsters, in 1977. She became the only woman ever to win a world championship in any form of motor sports. Several other women are trying in USAC, NASCAR, SCCA, and many smaller associations.

(Chan Bush photo)

Shirley Muldowney is the only woman ever to win a World Championship in motor sports.

USAC Cars and Tracks

The largest single sporting event in the world, in history, is a USAC race. At that one race are gathered more spectators than at any other event. More people are said to watch the race on TV than any other event. It is true that the race would be difficult to beat for spectacle, sound, color, and sheer drama.

You know which race it is. It is the famous Indianapolis Speedway Race. It is a 500-mile race on an oval track held every year on or about Memorial Day, in Indiana.

Some people still persist in calling the town "Indian-No-Place" and making fun of it. They say nothing else ever happens there. Nothing else *need* ever happen there. The 500-mile race alone would make up for a year of peace and calm and "nothing" happening. But, in fact, the largest NHRA drag race of the year is also held annually in Indianapolis, as are many other events and attractions.

The Indy 500 is a wild spectacle. Hundreds of thousands of people jam the town as race day approaches. On race morning, all lanes of traffic but one (for outgoing emergency vehicles), on every street and road leading to the track, are filled with cars. Some people have been camping in their cars for days to be one of the first into the giant infield (inside the track rather than in the grandstands outside). In this way they can rush to their favorite spot.

Most sports experts agree that nothing tops the sheer nerve-racking tension of 33 of the fastest racers in the world thundering into the first turn at Indy together as the race gets underway. Sometimes all 33 do not make it. Some years a car or driver will fail and pandemonium results. Once-perfect and shining race cars are instantly turned to junk as they carom off each other and the walls. Spectators have been hurt, and worse, as cars crash at Indy. Many, many drivers have died.

The USAC-CART "Indy-type" racer, known as a Championship Car, is a rear-engine, low-slung, open-wheel, open-cockpit missile. The driver is strapped in almost flat on his back, wearing a fire-resistant suit and helmet. There was a time when the Indy racer was a heavy, front-engine "roadster" type of car. Along came the Europeans with smaller, lighter, more spindly-looking cars with the engines in the back.

The foreign cars did very well at the biggest American race. Soon American drivers were trying the new lightweight cars. Today's Indy racer is somewhere between the little foreign car and the old American roadster. It has the engine in the rear and is low and flat and sleek. It is built especially to turn left, not right, on oval tracks (though, of course, it will turn right at slower speeds).

Like the Formula One racer, the Indy-type racer is a car built for one particular type of racing. But like many other racers, it has wide, flat, smooth tires with no tread. This gives the tire a larger "footprint," the

(Ross R. Olney photo)

The USAC-CART Indy-type racer, known as a Champion-ship Car, is a rear-engine, low-slung, open-wheel, open-cockpit missile with a turbocharger between the rear wheels. This is the car of Roger Mears, whose brother Rick won the 1979 Indy 500.

area where the tire meets the racing surface. Since the tire has no tread, Indy-type races are never held in the rain. The tires just slide when the track gets wet.

The Indy racer races at many tracks though. There are three 500-mile races on 2½-mile tracks every year. There is one at Indianapolis, one at Ontario Motor

Speedway in California, and one at Pocono, Pennsylvania.

The Indy-type car also races at smaller tracks of one and one half miles and even one mile. These tracks are scattered around the country. They are paved and usually oval in shape (Phoenix International Raceway, for example, is oval but has a "dogleg" indentation on the rear straightaway).

When USAC or CART races at Milwaukee, they use a one-mile paved oval. The same is true when they race at Trenton, New Jersey, and several other tracks.

USAC even takes their Championship racers to England to race. This is a treat for English racing fans, who are more accustomed to seeing formula-type cars (Formula One, Two, etc.). Of course the formula cars are similar to the Indy-type Championship car. The difference is that the formula cars are lighter, with less power, and are designed to be raced on a road course.

Most USAC Indy-type racers are unique in another respect. To the non-fan, racing cars look alike. But the Indy car has something that none of the others have. It is easy to see if you know what to look for. Even though all of these larger race cars have four big wheels, an open cockpit, wings, and an engine in the rear, you can instantly identify an Indy car because of this device.

It is a turbocharger. This is a unit attached to the exhaust pipe of the engine. It is round and has pipes going in and coming out.

A better view of a turbocharger (the upper rear unit with the air intake and the two exhaust openings) on A. J. Foyt's car. Foyt is to the right, inspecting the test tires. Racing tires are smooth, with no tread at all.

The hot, pressurized exhaust gases normally blasting from the exhaust pipe are guided into the turbocharger. Instead of escaping, they are directed over vanes that are soon turning at a high rate of speed (just like a windmill in a hurricane). The turning vane spins a shaft that is attached to another vane. This second one blows fresh air out of the turbocharger under high pressure.

But not out into the air. The fresh, pressurized air is blown back along another pipe and directly into the engine again. The extra air being forced into the engine creates very high pressures inside, increasing the power of the engine.

Some cars have a device in the cockpit that allows the driver to control the turbocharger "boost" (or amount of pressure). He can move a lever and allow more or less forced air into the engine. The more forced air that goes in, the higher the power—but the more likely the engine is to explode. The less forced air into the engine, the lower the power—but the longer the engine will probably live.

The strategy of setting the boost adjustment just right is critical in Indy-type racing. Watch for this turbocharger device on an Indy car's engine.

Many USAC race cars do not have turbochargers. Some fans insist that these cars are the purest race cars of all. They say these racers are what racing is really all about. Many insist that the only real racing in the world is done by USAC dirt cars, sprint cars, and midgets.

Most often they race on dirt tracks. The tracks are usually quarter- or half-mile ovals. They are scattered around the country by the hundreds. Dozens of smaller

(Photo courtesy of J. C. Agajanian)

Some fans say that racing midgets like these is the purest form of auto racing.

associations are involved in sprint and midget racing, and so is USAC.

All three types of car are similar in appearance. They are open-wheel, open-cockpit cars of the classic old race car shape. The engine is almost always in front and the cars have sloping rears where the fuel tanks are housed. The dirt car, called a dirt championship car, is the largest. It is very much like what used to be raced at Indianapolis years ago. Then comes the somewhat

Others would claim that distinction for this championship dirt-car type, here being driven by Mario Andretti.

smaller sprint car, and finally the smallest one, the midget. All three of these cars are fast, furious, exciting to watch, and very dangerous to drive.

A field of sprints or midgets snarling into a turn, all bunched together and skidding in four-wheel drifts, is thrilling to watch. Each racer is throwing a great fan of dirt from spinning, digging rear wheels. Very often, at least once or twice in each race, a midget or sprint car will spin out of control. Sometimes it will bounce and flip down the track and even over the fence.

Once a sprint car flipped through the fence at a track

116

in California. On the other side of the fence was a deep gulley. The race was at night. It took track workers over twenty minutes to locate the car. They only found it when the stunned driver regained his senses and called out. But even this was not as bad as the race car that bounced over a track fence and onto an empty flatcar in a passing train. The driver didn't see the rest of the race, for the train went another hundred miles before anybody knew enough to stop it.

In spite of the wild crashes, sprint car, dirt car, and midget car drivers are seldom injured, but sometimes they are. Midgets and sprints are considered to be the American training ground for drivers heading for the big USAC or CART races. If European Formula One drivers work their way up to the top through Formula Three and Two, then Americans work up to Championship cars through midgets and sprints. Many famous American drivers came up this way, though some did not. The great A. J. Foyt, the winningest driver in American racing history, started in midgets and sprints.

It is a tough road, though, and many young American drivers are lost along the way due to injury or death.

You can even start in quarter or three-quarter midget racing. These little cars look just like sprints or midgets, but they are smaller. They are very popular for amateur drivers who want to get the feel of "real" racing. They are also an excellent training ground for serious race drivers.

USAC sanctions a Bosch Mini-Indy series for Super

USAC also has a land speed record division for all-out speed attempts at the Salt Flats. This is the Challenger of Mickey Thompson. With four Pontiac engines, it set a new land speed record for piston-driven cars.

Vee racers. These cars are just like the cars in SCCA's Gold Cup series. In fact, it is often the very same cars and drivers.

Finally, USAC has a Land Speed Division for supervising and timing the world land speed record attempts at such places as Bonneville Salt Flats in Utah.

Why Drivers Drive in Any Association

Associations control and manage auto racing. They make the rules and see that the rules are followed.

There are many, many more associations and clubs than the ones mentioned in this book.

Racing associations can be difficult to deal with, for they try to rule their part of the sport with an iron hand. Whether it is a local group controlling local racing or a worldwide group involved in world racing, they are jealous of their turf. They want no trespassers.

The associations are a necessary part of modern auto racing. Without them, racing would be even more disorganized than it is. Everybody would be drifting.

Togetherness, in fact, must be very important to auto racing people. Racers who chose not to join certain sanctioning groups became known as "outlaws." They wanted to race, but they wanted to do so on their own terms. A few of them became well known in the racing world because of their skill on the track.

So a "World of Outlaws" race was organized. It featured the non-joining drivers. The non-joiners had joined together in an association of their own.

Associations are important for other reasons besides rule-making and policing. They collect the money and pay out the prizes. In each particular field, they have made driver safety important. From back when Wally Parks pushed through rules on roll bars for racing roadsters, safety has been an important part of every club's function.

Most associations now insist that their drivers wear full fire suits (fire-resistant coveralls, hood, gloves, socks, and boots, over fire-resistant underwear). Helmets are required. Roll-bar regulations are strict. Most associations provide corner workers, fire fighters, medical people, ambulances, and many other safety items.

One of the most important keys to the success of motor racing in the United States (more people watch races than watch football, basketball, baseball, or any other sport but horse racing) has been competition on the track and between associations. It would seem that with FIA running FISA, FISA running ACCUS-FIA, Inc., and ACCUS-FIA, Inc., running the four major U.S. clubs, things would be orderly and smooth. But there is competition.

USAC, who always handled oval track racing, began sanctioning road races. This cut into SCCA's territory. Meanwhile, USAC battled CART for Championship races.

SCCA has always been more amateur road race, sports car oriented. They moved into professional races with Can Am, Trans Am, and other pro series for big, heavy, brute race cars similar in many ways to USAC's Indy cars.

NASCAR always controlled stock car racing in the United States, but now USAC has a stock car division with rules almost identical to NASCAR's. Of course SCCA has always had some stock classes. Both SCCA and USAC sanction Super Vee races, often with the very same cars and drivers.

NHRA is not bothered by USAC, SCCA, or NASCAR, but they do have strong competition from IHRA and AHRA.

Smaller sedans like the Camaro and the Mustang were always sanctioned by SCCA in road races. Now NASCAR has some series for these cars. USAC has invaded this territory, too.

NASCAR now sanctions road races for big, heavy stock cars, and so does USAC. Smaller racing clubs have smaller territories to oversee. A club may be formed with but two or three tracks. Each of these tracks, under the guidance of the club, runs by the same rules. They may race any one of the types of cars normally sanctioned by the larger clubs but maybe under somewhat

Super Vee racing is a step up from Vee racing. A VW engine is used, but many racing modifications are allowed in the body and suspension. These cars race in Mini Indy (USAC) and Gold Cup (SCCA) racing.

relaxed rules. Perhaps they won't meet the rigid safety standards of the larger clubs. Or, more likely, they may have some strictly local modification permitted—wings on sprint cars, figure-8 racing, or "destruction derby" type racing.

In spite of it all, auto racing is probably more "together" than many other sports. In certain aspects, at least. For one thing, auto racing has its International Race of Champions.

"Who is the best driver of all?" fans began to ask several years ago. "Given equal cars, and no matter what type of racing they normally do, which driver is best?"

The IROC (International Race of Champions) was created to answer the question. In equally prepared cars of exactly the same type (usually a stock-type racing sports car to equalize the difference between the different types of racing), drivers from around the world compete. Europeans are invited and so are Americans from the major racing clubs. Twelve drivers usually race in a series of three races on three different-type tracks. Cars are selected by draw, so that everything is as equal as possible.

The results of these races, held over the past few years, have been inconclusive. Each year, it seems, the over-all winner comes from a different type of racing.

More important to auto racing than the IROC is the fact that a mechanic from Broken Buckle, Montana, can communicate with a mechanic at Nürburgring in

Auto racing has an International Race of Champions where twelve of the top drivers in the world compete in identical cars.

Germany in a common language. Fans of fast cars can see the beauty of a sleek Formula One at Watkins Glen and a thundering stocker at Daytona. Thus they understand each other. Drivers understand the love of racing, from a Sunday afternoon racer in a Formula Vee to a Grand Prix champion or an Indy winner.

Once, after a world Grand Prix race at Long Beach, California, former FIA World Driving Champion Jackie Stewart found himself alone on the street. He had been

Anything can happen at an IROC race, where all the super-stars gather. NASCAR's Richard Petty (left) laughs as Formula One driver Jody Scheckter takes the hat and microphone of former World Champion Jackie Stewart (right) and attempts an interview.

covering the race as a "color" man for television. His rental car, having been parked in a zone later declared to be illegal, had been towed away. He and his family were temporarily stranded.

Along came a young amateur driver from the SCCA Formula Vee class. This is the beginning class, said to be the cheapest form of motor racing. The amateur offered the best driver in the world a lift to where his car had been impounded. The drive took half an hour.

Was conversation general? About the weather? The recently completed race? The towed-away sedan?

The conversation between the two drivers was about racing. It was give and take, advice offered and quickly accepted. How to take a corner. How to learn most quickly. How to drive a fast car in competition. And about memories of driving at the beginning.

There was no apparent class distinction. The two, a beginner and a famous expert, discussed their mutual passion.

The associations may squabble, but they are necessary in order to control and to channel racing. They make it fair and even and competitive. They stumble, but they keep at it.

Fans and drivers and mechanics understand. They know control is necessary. They worry as little about it as possible, though. Meanwhile, they find their own common ground in friendship and camaraderie—and danger—and remain the main reason why motor racing in the United States and around the world continues to be one of the most popular sports of all.

Index

Italics indicate illustration

126

Rutherford, Johnny, 55

SCORE International, 22, 62, 74, 100
Scheckter, Jody, *18, 93, 124*
Shaw Gilmore Special, *8*
Shaw, Wilbur, *8, 36*
Sneva, Tom, 55, *72*
Southern California Timing Association (SCTA), 47–48
Sports Car Club of America (SCCA), 21–23, 27, 36–46, 58, 60, 68, 73, 83–100, 108, 120–121
sprint car, *58*, 114
Stewart, Jackie, 93, 123–124, *124*

Tambay, Patrick, 92
Thompson, Dannie, *63*
Thompson, Mickey, *63, 118*
turbocharger, 112–114

United States Auto Club (USAC), 12–15, *21*, 22–23, 52–59, 61, 68, 73–74, 82, 100, 108–118, 120–121
Unser, Al, *26*

Vukovich, Bill, *59*
Vukovich, Bill "Mad Russian," 59

Walther, Salt, *56*
Waltrip, Darrell, 34
Ward, Roger, *57*
World Driving Champion, 18–19, *20*, 46, 55, 93
World Kart Association, 65
World of Outlaws, 119

Yarborough, Cale, 34–35, 79

Zimmerman, Dick, *67*